A Break in the Ocean Cable

Maurice Scollard Baldwin

old books. new life.

A Break

IN THE

Ocean Cable.

————— ◆ —————

BY

MAURICE S. BALDWIN, M.A.

Rector of the Parish of Montreal, and Canon of the Cathedral.

————— ◆ —————

MONTREAL:

DAWSON BROTHERS, PUBLISHERS.

1877.

A BREAK IN THE OCEAN CABLE.

Let us imagine that, by some accident, all the cables now uniting Europe and America were suddenly to break. What a complete disarrangement of all our plans would such a calamity cause! Not only could no message on that day be transmitted from either side, but for weeks, and perhaps months, there could be no exchange of ideas, except through the tedious medium of the post. Two worlds must wait until the injury is repaired. In the meantime anxious people, on either side the water, would find the suspension of intelligence unbearable. Yesterday we could literally converse with our absent friends in London, Paris, or Berlin; to-day, as far as news from them is concerned, all is silent as the grave. Europe, with her mighty capitals, is still beyond the sea; her countless factories, and her Babel voices are still making the air vocal with the sounds

of busy life.   But of all this we have no imme-
diate evidence.   No wire flashes to us the
longed-for intelligence from distant relatives or
friends; no message, instantaneously communicated, makes us feel as though hands had clasped.
All that we can see or hear is the illimitable
ocean, with its restless waters, ebbing and
flowing for ever.

Now, it is exactly the same with thousands
in their spiritual relations to God.   In nothing
do they more firmly believe than in all the grand
verities of the Christian religion.   They believe
that Jesus died, and rose again; that He ascended
into Heaven, and is now seated at the Father's
right hand in glory; and yet, notwithstanding
all this, they are conscious that no life whatever
flows from God into their hearts.   The sweet
peace which comes from being justified by
faith; the joy which results from the indwelling
of the Comforter; the strong assurance which
anticipates victory before the battle is fought:
of all these blessed fruits of the Spirit, they know
absolutely nothing, and the reason is:—

The spiritual and vital COMMUNION *which
once existed between* GOD *and* MAN, *and which,
like a* CABLE, *bound Creator and creature together,
has, by the* UNBELIEF *of man, been* SEVERED.

The utter want, therefore, of peace and joy and life, from which those of whom I speak suffer, is the result of this terrible rupture; and so long as it remains unrepaired, that unrest and that death must inevitably continue. This may be the very case, dear reader, with you. The joy of believers is not *your* joy; *their* hope not *your* hope. Your whole happiness, all you have within the limits of time, is staked on the beating of your heart, and that *may* cease now, and is *sure* to do so hereafter; and yet you are indifferent about your soul, about eternity, about God. Perhaps this indifference astonishes *you*; I am sure it wearies the long-suffering of *God.* If you ask me why it is so—why you have not the joy and peace and love that Christians have? I can only answer: The ¦CABLE that should -UNITE you to GOD is BROKEN, and until it is repaired in the way laid down by God in Holy Scripture, the spiritual death in which your soul now lies, will be perpetuated into eternity.

By the *cable*, then, I understand that spiritual and visible communion which once existed between God and man, and which can now only be restored through personal faith in the Lord Jesus Christ. Broken it now is, and so completely, that no communication can possibly take place while it is in this state. Joy and peace only come to the soul when it is in communion with God ; in order, therefore, dear reader, that you may become thus united to the Father through the Lord Jesus Christ, let me draw your attention to *two* questions, connected with the subject, of the deepest moment to us all.

First :—HOW WAS THE CABLE BROKEN ?

Second :—HOW IS IT TO BE REPAIRED ?

In considering the first question—" How was the cable broken "—the Scriptures teach us that there was a time when man was in direct and constant communication with God ; when God spoke freely to him, and he to God ; when the joy of Heaven was man's joy, and all that God expected of man, *that* he hasted to yield ; when sin, which has since brought such fearful havoc into the world, was unknown to him, then was his peace as a river, and his righteousness as the waves of the sea. He saw God walking amid the bowers of Eden ; he knew His gracious voice ; he believed His word ; he obeyed His commands. God was

> " The spring of all his joys,"
> " The life of his delights,"
> " The glory of his brightest day,"
> " And comfort of his nights."

Such was man's state during that short, but happy period, in which he walked in sinless obedience to God.

The one great characteristic of that most blessed life was—implicit FAITH in God's word. Our first parents, in their holy innocence, believed most sincerely, loved most fervently, and obeyed most faultlessly, all that God either promised or enjoined.

Now, as being absolutely essential to their *own* happiness, and to that of the countless millions who were to come after them, God positively required of them both that they should believe in a sentence of DEATH THREATENED. The sentence itself was as follows:—

"THE TREE OF THE KNOWLEDGE OF GOOD AND EVIL, THOU SHALT NOT EAT OF IT: FOR IN THE DAY THOU EATEST THEREOF, THOU SHALT SURELY DIE."—Gen. ii. 17.

Not only their happiness, but their *life itself* depended on their implicit faith in this most solemn utterance of God. And, therefore, so long as they did believe, and as a consequence, obeyed the Divine command, their peace flowed on uninterruptedly. Eden was their home, and

God their Father and their Friend. This state, moreover, of perfect blessedness, might have remained to man until this day, for God, in His great love, had only restricted him in one particular:—he was not to eat of the forbidden fruit. If he disobeyed, inevitable death was to be the consequence. Joy, peace, life, everything in fact, depended on their believing in this threatened sentence of death. All else that God had said was affirmative; this was the ONE negative: "Thou shalt *not* eat of it, for in the day thou eatest thereof thou shalt surely die." The reason, therefore, that Adam and Eve abstained from eating the forbidden fruit, was, they BELIEVED: when they no longer believed, they DISOBEYED.

RUPTURE OF THE CABLE.

Our great adversary, Satan, now appears upon the scene. He comes in the form of a serpent, and thus addresses Eve:—" Yea, hath God said, ye shall not eat of every tree of the garden?" This is his first effort to introduce sin into the world. He does not, in this advance, even attempt to deny the truthfulness of God's word; he only endeavours to inject into Eve's mind a doubt as to whether God ever uttered any such prohibition at all. He asks:—" Yea, *hath* God said ?" As if he would say, " Are you perfectly sure about this matter ?" The temptation, insidious as it was, failed. Eve was *sure* as to the prohibition. She replied, " We may eat of the fruit of the trees of the garden ; but of the fruit of the tree which is in the midst of the garden, God hath said, ' Ye shall not eat of it, neither shall ye touch it, lest ye die.'" Finding this effort thus abortive, Satan now advances boldly to deny God's word itself:—" Ye shall not surely die," he says, " for God doth know that in the day ye eat thereof, then your eyes shall be opened, and ye shall be as gods, knowing good and evil." Here, then, were *two* statements before Eve :—

God's : " THOU SHALT SURELY DIE."
Satan's : " THOU SHALT NOT SURELY DIE."

Up to this time, Eve had implicitly believed God's statement; she now hesitates, trembles, and then finally accepts Satan's.

The deed was done ; for though she had not yet committed that high-handed act of disobedience, by which many were made sinners, and by which death was brought into the world, yet she had let spring into existence that terrible principle of UNBELIEF; from which disobedience resulted as its natural and legitimate fruit. First Eve, and then Adam, *distrusted* God. They believed, though they had God's own word directly to the contrary, that the eating of the forbidden fruit would ameliorate their condition. It would make them, so the serpent said, as gods, knowing good and evil. *Then* it was the GREAT CABLE BROKE! Man *distrusting* God; doubting Him, who is the TRUTH itself.

The next question is:—HOW IS THE CABLE TO BE REPAIRED?

When the Atlantic cable snaps, ships are immediately sent to find out, if possible, where the break occurred. Sometimes, with incredible labour, the cable is raised, only to find they must go further; but when at last they have firmly grappled the two broken ends, their work is virtually done, for that which remains is so easy of accomplishment, that it need cause them no anxiety.

Now, precisely similar to this is the case of the great spiritual cable: where its BREAK occurred, there only can its parts be RE-JOINED.

It would be of no avail for electricians to add plate to plate to their battery, in the fond hope that thus they could drive a message through the entire length of the broken cable. Only one way is open to them, and that is, to find out *where* the fault is, and *there* make the mend. Thus also is it with man in his spiritual relation to God. *Where* the spiritual cable broke, *there* only can its parts be re-joined.

Now we have just learned that the cable was severed by UNBELIEF. The teaching of Scripture is—it can only be united by FAITH.

In order, however, that the reader may see more clearly God's way of peace, I will now place before him, both the *break* and the *re-joining* :—

First,—THE BREAK.

God asked man, in the Garden of Eden, to believe in a SENTENCE OF DEATH THREATENED. Man would not. On the contrary, he accepted a lying statement that he would NOT die, and that his condition generally would be much bettered by his sin. This led to his high-handed act of disobedience in plucking the forbidden fruit. The BREAK, however, occurred through his UNBELIEF.

Second—THE RE-JOINING.

God now puts LIFE *first*. Instead, therefore, of asking men *first* to believe " *in a sentence of*

DEATH *threatened*," He commands us to believe in *everlasting life*, GOD'S GIFT, *through Jesus Christ our Lord*.

Now, in both these cases, God asks of man exactly the same condition—IMPLICIT FAITH IN HIS WORD. The difference lies in this :—In the *first* instance, man had only DEATH brought before him; in the *second* he has GOOD TIDINGS OF ETERNAL LIFE.

To-day, life, glorious, unending life, is offered to the WORLD, and the whole world is bidden take it as a GIFT. A little while ago, and God, pointing to a tree, said : " In the day that thou eatest thereof, thou shalt surely die." *To-day*, pointing to a fairer and better tree, the tree of life, He says : " The leaves of this tree are 'for the healing of the nations." " He that eateth of this Bread shall live for ever." God does *not* say there is no death, but He affirms it will *only* be inflicted where there is an actual rejection of Christ. " He that believeth and is baptized, shall be saved ; but he that believeth not, shall be damned."—Mark xvi. 16.

To obtain, however, a thoroughly clear idea of the mode by which the RE-JOINING is to be effected, *two* things are absolutely necessary :—

First: We should understand what Scriptural teaching is, concerning our Lord Jesus Christ.

Second: We should also know what is meant by "*Faith in the Son of God.*"

As regards the *first* of these two most import-ant points, the Holy Scriptures teach :—

(a) *The Lord Jesus Christ has been exalted to be the Saviour of the world.*

Speaking to the Son, the Father says: " It is a light thing that Thou shouldest be my servant to raise up the tribes of Jacob, and to restore the preserved of Israel: I will also give Thee for a light to the Gentiles, that Thou mayest be my SALVATION unto the END of the EARTH."—Isaiah xlix. 6.

" Look unto ME, and be ye SAVED, all the ENDS OF THE EARTH: for I am God, and there is none else."—Isaiah xlv. 22.

Appointing Paul as His apostle to the Gen-tiles, our Lord thus addresses him :— * * * " The GENTILES unto whom now I send thee, to open *their* eyes and to turn them from darkness to light, and from the power of Satan unto God, that *they* may receive forgiveness of sins, and INHERITANCE among them which are sanctified by faith that is in Me."—Acts xxvi. 17, 18.

"This is the will of Him that sent Me, that every one which seeth the Son, and believeth on Him, may have EVERLASTING LIFE."—John vi. 40.

"And we have seen, and do testify that the Father sent the SON to be the SAVIOUR of the WORLD."—1 John, iv. 14.

(b) *That this honour of being the Saviour of the world is accorded to* NONE OTHER.

St. Peter, "filled with the Holy Ghost," thus bore witness to the Lord Jesus Christ before the elders of the Jews:—" This is the stone which was set at nought of you builders, which is become the Head of the corner; neither is there salvation IN ANY OTHER: for there is NONE OTHER NAME under Heaven given among men whereby we must be saved."—Acts iv. 11, 12.

(c) *That Christ became the Saviour of the world by virtue of* HIS DEATH ON THE CROSS.

"He was wounded for our transgressions; He was bruised for our iniquities; the chastisement of our peace was UPON HIM, and with HIS STRIPES we are HEALED."—Isaiah liii. 5.

* * * "Jesus our Lord, * * who was DELIVERED for our offences, and was raised again for our justification."—Rom. iv. 24, 25.

"Who GAVE HIMSELF for our sins, that He might deliver us from this present evil world, according to the will of God and our Father."—Gal. i. 4.

"Christ hath redeemed us from the curse of the law, being made A CURSE FOR US: for it is written, Cursed is every one that hangeth on a tree."—Gal. iii. 13.

"Who, being in the form of God, thought it not robbery to be equal with God: but made Himself of no reputation, and took upon Him the form of a servant, and was made in the likeness of men: and being found in fashion as a man, He humbled Himself, and became OBEDIENT UNTO DEATH, even the DEATH OF THE CROSS. Wherefore God also hath highly exalted Him, and given Him a name which is above every name: that at the name of JESUS every knee should bow, of things in Heaven, and things in earth, and things under the earth."—Phil. ii. 6, 7, 8, 9, 10.

"Who His own self bore our sins IN HIS OWN BODY ON THE TREE, that we being dead to sins, should live unto righteousness: by whose STRIPES ye were HEALED."—1 Peter, ii 24.

The song which John heard sung in heaven by the four " living creatures," and by the four and twenty Elders, was as follows:—" Thou art worthy to take the book, and to open the seals thereof: for thou wast SLAIN, and hast redeemed us to God by THY BLOOD out of every kindred, and tongue, and people, and nation."—Rev. v. 9.

We now come to the consideration of the *second point, namely, Scripture teaching concerning* FAITH *in our Lord Jesus Christ.*

First, I would have you notice that *the people who are called upon to believe are the* SPIRITUALLY DEAD. Untold thousands go astray here. They are sure they must DO something in order to be saved; whereas the dead can DO NOTHING. They fancy they must first *merit* salvation before God will grant it; and this they propose to effect by a thorough change of life in thought, word and deed. Should they ever accomplish so great a result, they believe that then they may, with all reason, sue for pardon and for peace. Now, what is the result of this terrible mistake? That days, and months, and years roll away; youth ripens into manhood, and manhood into old age, and yet the anticipated change never takes place. The heart grows harder, or remains as unchanged as the rocks they tread upon. Even those who have tried a thousand times to do all this, and failed in every effort, will often still persist in believing that it can be accomplished, if only they are *more* persistent. It is an utter impossibility. " Can the Ethiopian," asks the Scripture, "change his skin, or the leopard his spots? then may ye also do good, that are accustomed to do evil."— Jer. xiii. 23. But people ask: "Why is this?" The answer is: All out of Christ are DEAD; and the dead can do NOTHING. "But may we not," ask they, "please God in *some* way or other, and thus obtain—if not life itself, at least a *mitigated sentence*? " For instance, by giving liberally to the poor— feeding the hungry—clothing the naked, and generally discharging all the obligations of life honourably—may we not please God, even if we be not personally united to the Lord Jesus Christ?" The answer to this question is, emphatically, NO. However costly the gift a man may offer to God—however great his sacrifice, or tremendous his effort—yet, if it be presented to God without faith in the Redeemer, so far from *pleasing* Him, IT IS A SIN. " Whatsoever is not of faith is sin."—Rom. xiv. 23.

" *Without faith*," says the Apostle Paul, " it is impossible to please Him."—Heb. xi. 6.

And again : " They that are in the flesh *cannot please God*."—Rom. viii. 8.

These works of mercy and of love, are unto God a " *sweet savour*," when done by those who are *in Christ*.   Indeed, believers are God's workmanship, created in Christ Jesus unto GOOD WORKS.   But out of Christ *nothing* is acceptable, for the dead cannot please God.   " If this be the case," say some, " are we to do NOTHING ?"   You can DO nothing ; you are LOST.   If you could do anything, you would not be lost.   Men who have been shipwrecked, and have taken to their boats, may be in an extremely perilous position, but they are *not lost*.   It is far different, however, with you, reader, if you are out of Christ: *you are lost*. The Lord Jesus Christ has said: " He that believeth not the Son, shall not *see life*, but the *wrath of God abideth on him*."—John iii. 36.

This, then, is the reason—the fact that all out of Christ are lost—why the great Redeemer announces that His mission was: *to save the* LOST.   " The Son of Man," He says, " is come to seek and to save that which was lost."— Luke, xix. 10.   But more than this, the *lost* are called the DEAD.

Our Lord, speaking of the glorious life which He bestows, says: "Verily, verily, I say unto you, the hour is coming, and NOW IS, when the DEAD shall hear the voice of the Son of God: and they that HEAR shall LIVE."—John, v. 25.

Of the believer, He affirms: "That he is passed from *death* unto *life*."—John, v. 24.

St. Paul also declares, in writing to the Ephesians: "And you hath he QUICKENED, who were DEAD in trespasses and sins."—Eph. ii. 1.

Secondly: That the Agency made use of by God the Holy Ghost, in the quickening of dead souls, is the WORD.

"Verily, verily, I say unto you, He that heareth My WORD, and believeth on Him that sent Me, hath everlasting life, and shall not come into condemnation; but is passed from death unto life."—John, v. 24.

"Of His own will begat He us with the *word of truth*."—James, i. 18.

"Being born again, not of corruptible seed, but of incorruptible, *by the word of God*, which liveth and abideth for ever."—1 Peter, i. 23.

St. Paul says, writing to the Corinthians: "In Christ Jesus I have begotten you *through the Gospel*."—1 Cor. iv. 15.

Our Lord says: "Now ye are clean *through the word* which I have spoken unto you."— John xv. 3.

Christ is said to have given Himself for the Church, " that He might sanctify and cleanse it with the washing of water by the WORD."— Eph. v. 26.

God, in His own wisdom, brought Saul to the knowledge of Himself, *by a miracle;* but His regular agency is His *word.* People are not, therefore, to expect miracles to be wrought in their favour. Many do; and the result is, they wait, and wait, for what never comes, and are thus eternally lost. No, dear reader, God gives only to the *world* what he gives to *you,* His WORD. And speaking of that Word, the Redeemer said: " THY WORD IS TRUTH."— John, xvii. 17.

Thirdly : The Word requires men to believe in the great PAST ACT *of the Lord Jesus Christ.*

The great *central* truth in connection with the Lord Jesus Christ, is—*His death upon the Cross;* witnessed to, and accepted by the Father, as the propitiation for sin, in that He raised Him from the dead. This is the *great past act* of the Lord Jesus Christ. When, therefore, a sinner is saved, it is not because of something which Christ is to do for him IN THE FUTURE, but in virtue of what he has done for him IN THE PAST.

Now, dear reader, what has Christ done for *you* in the past? You reply: "He died for me." 'True; but are you now—*at this very moment*, saved? "No," you say, "but I hope hereafter to be so." Now, here it is you are astray, and this is the point to which I wish to bring you. Is it possible that Jesus died for you *in the past*, and that you can only be saved *in the future*? If you were in prison for debt, and a friend came and announced that he had paid every debt, and held a receipt from every creditor, surely you would then understand you had nothing to do but to go forth at once and show your gratitude to your friend. "But," you say, "the two cases are wholly different. In the case of the prison, the receipts would shew me, as well as every one else, I was free; but in the matter of my soul, I surely *have* something to do. I have, for instance, to show God how deep is my sorrow for my past sins; I have to cry earnestly to Him for pardon and peace; and then, when I prove to Him, by my renewed life and incessant prayers, that I am thoroughly sincere, He will, I know, for Christ's sake, forgive me." Now, here it is you *utterly*.

misunderstand the whole Gospel of Jesus Christ. Let me refer you to the Prophet Isaiah. In one verse he gives a complete summary of the Gospel:—" All we, like sheep, have gone astray; we have turned every one to his own way; and the Lord hath *laid on* HIM *the iniquity of* US ALL."—Isaiah, liii. 6.

Here, then, dear reader, your guilt was laid. There is no other offering for sin. HE was wounded for *our* transgressions; HE was bruised for *our* iniquities; the chastisement of *our* peace was upon HIM; and with HIS *stripes we are* HEALED."—Isaiah, liii. 5.

"Without *shedding of blood* is no *remission*."—Heb. ix. 22. But the Blood that cleanseth from guilt has been shed ALREADY. God asks for NOTHING more; only your acceptance of this great truth by simple *faith*. He requires no *moral* qualification whatever in you. You are spiritually dead, and Christ is your resurrection and life, to raise you from death. No, dear reader, if God had left the least thing to be done by you, there could be *no hope*. It is a small thing to change a switch on a railway; but if an advancing train is expecting that little to be done by one, who, at the time, is lying a corpse by the road-side, the train must inevitably be wrecked. So, too, if God left you, a spiritually dead man, until such time as you could fit yourself for salvation, your eternal doom would be settled. On the contrary, He brings you, and all the world of the unsaved, up to the Cross of Christ; and pointing to His Son, says : "Behold the Lamb of God, which taketh away the sin of the world."

And now, I fancy the reader saying : "But what does this faith mean ?" It means nothing else than the complete RE-JOINING of the BROKEN CABLE. God asks you, dear reader, to believe, not only that your sins were laid on the Lord Jesus Christ, but that the Saviour made a full satisfaction for them on the Cross. If you believe this, you are SAVED. Hear His word :—" God so loved the world, that He gave His only begotten Son, that WHOSOEVER BE-LIEVETH IN HIM should not perish, but have EVERLASTING LIFE."—John. iii. 16. Again, in the same Gospel, our Lord says : " Verily, verily, I say unto you, he that HEARETH my words, and BELIEVETH on Him that sent Me, HATH everlasting life, and shall not come into con-demnation; but IS passed from DEATH unto LIFE."—John, v. 24. It is not that you are to make some *future treaty* with God by prayers and supplications ; God points you to Christ on the Cross, and says:—*Believe, and live.* " By grace are ye saved, *through faith*; and that not of yourselves; it is the *gift of God.*"—Eph. ii. 8.

Observe, it is *not* a *promise* of life: it is *present* life. "Verily, verily, I say unto you, He that believeth on Me HATH everlasting Life."—John, vi. 47. It is not faith in *feeling*: it is faith *in Christ.* Many say: "O, I cannot *feel* that I am saved." God does not ask you to *feel*: He asks you to *believe* simply in HIS WORD. Feelings will follow in God's time.

Dear reader, I entreat you to take this life. You have not to cry aloud, and implore God to give you this blessed salvation. He gives it as a GIFT to all who believe in His dear Son. "The wages of sin is death: but THE GIFT OF GOD is eternal life, through Jesus Christ our Lord."—Rom. vi. 23. Now, if a friend offers you a gift, you do not begin to ask him to bestow it; you simply thank him for his kindness. And exactly thus is it with God. He offers you life as His GIFT. Take it, then, and praise Him for His love.

Fourthly: Faith comes from HEARING *God's word.*

What Eve disbelieved, was God's word; what God asks you *now* to believe is His word. The common idea with people is, they must *do* something to be saved; whereas God's plan is simply that they should HEAR and BELIEVE.

The Jews, we are told, came to our Lord, and said: "What shall we do, that we might work the works of God?" Jesus answered and said unto them: "THIS IS THE WORK OF GOD, THAT YE BELIEVE ON HIM WHOM HE HATH SENT."—John, vi, 29.

Faith is said by the Apostle Paul to be "The gift of God."—*Eph.* ii. 8. He tells us also how that gift is bestowed; and his information on this point comes as the deduction from all his previous reasoning: "So then, FAITH cometh by HEARING, and hearing by the WORD OF GOD."—Rom. x. 17. Faith, then, comes from the simple hearing of God's word, which is the blessed declaration of His will.

Here then, dear reader, is life eternal placed before you. The Saviour, pointing to the uplifted serpent in the wilderness, said: "EVEN SO must the Son of Man be lifted up: that whosover believeth in Him should not perish, but have eternal life." He spake of a life which is communicated as *instantaneously* as it is *freely.* It is given, not merely *without money*, but absolutely *without delay.*

"*As Moses lifted up the serpent in the wilderness,* EVEN SO *must the Son of Man be lifted up.*" And how, think you, dear reader, was Christ lifted up, so as to resemble the serpent of brass? Surely not when He was exalted above the Heavens, but when He hung upon the tree. Pointing you to that awful sacrifice, God says: BELIEVE and LIVE. Not that it *will* save you, provided only *you* do this or that, but that, being God's eternal satisfaction for sin, it does NOW save you, the very MOMENT you accept it by FAITH Faith, then, in the Lord Jésus Christ, is accepting this truth; it is believing that the Redeemer bore ALL your sins, and received their WHOLE PUNISHMENT in His own body on the tree. God asks nothing more; He will receive nothing less. This satisfied the FATHER, for He raised Him from the dead to show the whole world how fully He accepted His work. It satisfied the SON, for, anticipating His death, He said: "I have glorified Thee on the earth: I have finished the work Thou gavest Me to do." It satisfied the HOLY GHOST, for ever since, to every saint of God, He has witnessed the saving efficacy of the BLOOD of Christ, What, therefore, satisfied the Father—what satisfied the Son—what satisfied the Holy Ghost—let this, dear reader, satisfy

YOU. Believe in what Christ did for you THEN, when He bowed His head and died, and you will be saved NOW.

Faith, in other words, is believing, not in YOURSELF, but in CHRIST—not a trusting in feelings, as in the memory of some past conversion, but in the BLOOD which satisfied Divine justice, the blood of our Lord Jesus Christ.

If, dear reader, you accept this statement, simply on the credibility of God's word, you will, at the moment of your acceptance, pass from DEATH unto LIFE—you will be SAVED And then, when this most blessed result has taken place, a wondrous change will be wrought in you.

First, *in your mind:* You will know you are saved, because you will have the simple statement of God's word to that effect. When a man accepts Christ, he knows he is saved, because *God's word says so.* The Redeemer said: "Verily, verily, I say unto you, he that believeth on Me *hath* everlasting life." Now, then, when I believe in Him, I know I am saved, because I know Him to be true. He has said: He that believeth *is* saved. I believe, *therefore* I KNOW *I am* saved. This is faith on God's *word.* It is not therefore dependent on

feeling or excitement of any kind; it rests on
that which is more stable than the eternal hills
—on the word of God itself.

Secondly, *in your life*: Then, at that very
moment when you believe, you will receive the
Holy Ghost; you will become one with Christ,
and Christ with you; your whole life will be
changed by this amazing union. The Scriptures
are very explicit on this point. St. Paul says:
"Therefore, if any man be in Christ, he is a NEW
CREATURE: old things are passed away; behold, all things are become NEW."—2 Cor. v. 17.
Then, and not till then, will you begin to work
for Christ, and your work will be acceptable to
Him. It will not be *dead*, but *living* work,
wrought through your vital union with the Lord
Jesus Christ. You will work, not that you *may*
be saved but because you *are* saved, and that
labor will be sweet.

Dear unsaved reader, delay not, for a single
moment, accepting this life. "NOW is the accepted time, NOW is the day of salvation." What
our first parents LOST through unbelief, namely,
life eternal, that do you ACCEPT, as GOD'S
GIFT, THROUGH FAITH IN JESUS CHRIST OUR
LORD.

THE QUICKENING OF THE BELIEVER.

And now I wish to say a few words to the BELIEVER, concerning his standing and walk in the Lord Jesus Christ.

First,—It is quite possible that, owing to the coldness and Laodicean state of your soul, the cable, even in *your* case, may be broken. I by no means wish to imply that you are in an utterly lost condition, as though you had never accepted Christ, or had been accepted by Him. That would be an utter impossibility, for the unalterable declaration of God's will is: "He that hath the Son HATH Life."—1 John v. 12. The blessing which the Redeemer bestows on His people is *Eternal Life.* "I give unto them *Eternal Life;* and they shall never perish, neither shall any man pluck them out of My hand."—John x. 28. God's gift is "*Eternal life* through Jesus Christ our Lord."—Rom. vi. 23. Such is the salvation of the Son of God—life eternal; not fading, evanescent life, coming and going, according to the moods and frames of our minds, but settled and fixed above all these *in the eternity* of the Lord Jesus Christ. The source of the believer's life is not *prayer*, nor *earnestness*, nor any faculty or energy within him; it is *hidden in the awful*

mystery of Christ's own being. "Because I LIVE,
YE shall LIVE also," (John xiv. 19.) is His own
definition of what our life is. Similar to this, is
the language of St. Paul:—"For ye are dead, and
your life is HID with CHRIST in GOD."
Col. iii. 3. Seeing, therefore, that such is the
teaching of Scripture, it behoves us to take no
lower ground, but rather honor Him the more
who is at once "our *way,* our TRUTH, our
LIFE."

Secondly,—In agreement with the above, is
the melancholy fact that some Christians are
utterly destitute of all spiritual joy and peace
in believing. They have no real communion with God—no testimony of the Spirit as to
their sonship; they are practically dead while
they live.

Now this is what I mean when I say: "Even
with the believer the cable may be broken." It
is *not* so really: it *is* so practically. This awful
state of spiritual declension has been brought
about by his not living *near* Christ; by allowing
the world, Satan and the flesh to obtain a
mastery over the soul, and thus a heavy cloud
has settled down upon it, hiding the Father's
face from him, and in this darkness of separa-
tion from God the poor believer exists. Bleak
winter is howling where tropical summer might

reign. Nothing can be more sad than such a state, because every hour that a believer continues out of communion with God, the Holy Spirit is grieved, the Saviour is slighted, and the Father's love wearied by the backsliding of His child.

Such are the people to whom our Lord addresses His most severe words of condemnation in his epistles to the churches—the Christians who shall be SAVED, but *so as by fire*—the Christians who doubtless will take A PLACE in the kingdom of God, but who will be there WITHOUT the glorious CROWN promised to the faithful in Christ Jesus.

Our blessed Lord in the 15th chapter of St. John, describes the effect of union with Himself thus:—"Every branch IN ME that beareth NOT fruit He taketh away: and every branch, that beareth fruit, He purgeth it, that it may bring forth more fruit."—John xv. 2. Now here the Redeemer states the result of his children failing to bring forth fruit. Fruit is that which God expects. St. Paul says: "We are His workmanship, created in Christ Jesus unto good works, which God hath before ordained that we should walk in them."—Eph. ii. 10. If therefore we do *not* bring forth fruit, God's order is perverted. We frustrate His high and holy purpose in calling us out of darkness into the Kingdom of his dear Son. The Saviour Himself is not indifferent *to the slight which is done Him* in this matter; He cannot, and will not, allow any dishonour shown to His name. "His eyes are as a flame of fire," "He walks amid the seven golden candlesticks," "He searcheth the reins and hearts." When therefore the Lord sees a branch unfruitful, judicial sentence must follow: God the Father, as the heavenly husbandman, takes that branch *away.* He removes it from the position it once held, *as being unworthy of His name.* He will not use it, and the result is—moral night settles over the soul, and DEATH, (as far as peace and joy are concerned) takes place, and in this awful declension many Christians remain. They are not actually dead, but they are in a *dead* state. They have no gladness in their hearts, for God in whose presence is fulness of joy, is not with them. He is not using them, He has taken them away from the position they once held, and therefore, immersed in the *cares,* and sometimes even in the *amusements* of this world, they drag on a miserable existence, insulting on the one hand to the love of God, and utterly destructive on the other to the peace and happiness of their own souls. How are such souls to be quickened? This is the question with which, in conclusion, we are solely concerned.

The answer Holy Scripture gives to this question is:—*The revival of their faith by a personal coming to the Lord Jesus Christ.*

To the Laodicean Christians who had gone back to such a fearful extent that they were "wretched, and miserable, and poor, and blind, and naked," Our Lord counselled that they should buy of Him "gold tried in the fire, that they might be rich; and white raiment, that they might be clothed, and that they should anoint their eyes with eye salve, that they might see."—Rev. iii. 18.

If you, dear reader, should be one of these, I would earnestly implore of you to draw near afresh to the Lord Jesus Christ, who is both able and willing to save you to the uttermost. And then, instead of spiritual poverty, you will have the gold which has been tried in the fire. Christ will be your portion. You will be complete in Him. Instead of nakedness, you will be clothed with His beauty. You will be made "THE RIGHTEOUSNESS OF GOD IN HIM." Instead of blindness, "the Lord shall be thine everlasting light, and the days of thy mourning shall be ended." Christ is indeed your portion now; if you are a child of God, and in Christ, most assuredly are you complete; but you will be brought into the *conscious enjoyment* of all these precious truths, and thus into full communion with God.

The great truth the believer has to bear in mind is this: "We walk by FAITH, not by SIGHT." 2. Cor. v. 7. This has especially to be considered in our ceaseless contest with sin, in its ever varying forms. We pray, (and no prayer could possibly be more needed) that God will completely subject the flesh to the spirit. Now I can hardly imagine a prayer more in accordance with Scripture than this, and yet I think many may be mistaken as to the way in which God will answer such a prayer when offered up to Him in lowly faith. We naturally rise from our knees thinking *henceforth* we shall be wholly *free* from all those thoughts, tempers and suggestions which, with a rapidity greater than that of lightning, rush into our minds and lead us into sin. Yet this idea is founded on a mistake. The flesh, which is IN us, is in hopeless *opposition* to God. "It is not *subject* to the law of God, neither indeed *can* be."—Rom. viii. 7. We have therefore *two* distinct natures absolutely and inherently opposed to each other, namely— that which is born of the Spirit, and which is, in the language of our Lord, spirit: and that which is born of the flesh, which *is* flesh. Observe, no depth of earnestness, or devotion to the cause of God will ever make the flesh spirit, or even *like* the spirit. To the end of the terrible contest, the "flesh," that is, the nature which we inherited from Adam, and which is called by St. Paul the "old man," will continue fiercely opposed to all the motions of the Spirit.

When therefore we pray that the "flesh" may be subjected to the Spirit, we pray that "sin should not *reign* in our mortal body, that we should obey it in the lusts thereof." That sin is within us, and *will* be in us to the end, is certain; but we are not to let it guide or influence us; we are not to let it REIGN in our hearts.

The question then presents itself: How are we to *prevent* it reigning there?—how are we to get the complete victory over it? I answer: By our Lord Jesus Christ; who is able to make us more than conquerors, "according to the working whereby He is ABLE even to SUBDUE ALL THINGS unto HIMSELF."

Now, we are most distinctly told by St. Paul, that "our old man" was crucified together with Christ. By the expression "our old man," he means the flesh, our natural carnal heart which we inherited from Adam. His language is as follows:—"Knowing this, that our old man is crucified with Him, that the body of sin might be destroyed, that henceforth we should not serve sin."—Rom. vi. 6. So also in the Epistle to the Galatians, the same apostle declares: "I am crucified with Christ."—Gal. ii. 20; or, as it is more literally translated, "I have been crucified (co-crucified) with Christ." The meaning of these most remarkable words is to be sought in the position Our Lord occupied as the *Representative* of His people. When Our Lord Jesus Christ died, He was not only the bearer of the sin of the world, but He was also the head and representative of all the redeemed. What therefore Christ did, His people are represented as having done also. Now, Our Lord died unto sin ONCE. In this death the believer participates; he is ONE with Christ in DEATH: As *Christ* died unto sin, so also did *he*, but in the person of His great representative. On the CROSS Christ died unto sin; on the Cross the BELIEVER DIED ALSO. "I have been co-crucified with Christ," said St. Paul; that is, "I have *with Christ* died unto sin." The "I" means all that the Apostle was by *nature*—himself in his natural unrenewed state. This, his carnal heart, the " old man " of Rom. vi. 6, died with His Lord on the Cross. Judicial sentence was then executed upon it: in the language of Scripture, IT DIED. But believers ask—how can the flesh have died, when we find its motions so strong in our hearts to-day? I answer: the "flesh" is *judicially dead*, because the sentence of death was executed on it when Christ our representative died. Observe the strong language of St. Paul:—"Knowing this that our old man was CRUCIFIED WITH HIM; that the body of sin might de DE-STROYED, that HENCEFORTH WE SHOULD NOT SERVE SIN." Here, then, is the glorious privilege of the believer—by his union with Christ in death, he is FREED from the dominion of sin. The Apostle says:—"He that hath DIED hath been SET FREE from sin."—Rom. vi. 7. (Alford.) The believer is now no longer compelled to *serve* sin; he is to reckon himself to be *dead* indeed unto sin, but *alive* unto God through Jesus Christ our Lord.

Two practical results flow from the just appreciation of this truth.

First,—In our conflict with *ourselves* we know that that which would lead us captive, if it could, namely, our natural carnal heart, has been CONDEMNED and CRUCIFIED with

Christ. In other words, we know our greatest enemy is not supreme; it is BENEATH the FEET of Christ. No *outside* enemy has half the power to injure our spiritual life as the wicked heart within. But this " wicked heart within " is beneath the power of Christ, our Deliverer and our God. Let us not, then, be discouraged, nor grow faint with weariness; however strong, however insidious the flesh may be, IT IS NOT OUR MASTER. Our Master is *Christ*, not the *flesh*. Why need I, then, be a CAPTIVE TO THE FLESH when I stand in the presence of Him who has OVERCOME THE FLESH, my Lord and Saviour Jesus Christ

Second,—This truth teaches us how to *regard* the motions of sin. Sin is by no means dead *in* the believer, but the believer is dead *to* sin. When, therefore, the passions of sin rise within you, reckon yourself DEAD to them. Give no place to them; and, turning to Him who has by His death freed you from the dominion of sin, realize your victory in Him. Then it is, He will make you MORE than a CONQUEROR. You will learn the meaning of this blessed assurance: "Sin shall not have dominion over you; for ye are not under the law, but UNDER GRACE."—Rom. vi. 14. Be not discouraged, then, about the presence of sin in you. That

which is " FLESH " will always CONTINUE
"flesh," even though you were to live a thousand
years on earth. Neither prayer, earnestness, nor
zeal, will ever change the flesh: it may be
SUBDUED ; it cannot be CHANGED. To the
end, therefore, it will maintain its character—
one of irreconcilable hostility to God. When
St. Paul says to the Corinthians : " If any man
be in Christ, he is a new creature," the Apostle
means, the man has been made a NEW CREA-
TION ; that is, a totally new life has been im-
parted to him, and this new life is the SPIRIT.
The new creation is not, therefore, the " flesh "
suddenly made holy—that were impossible—but
a NEW SPIRIT, begotten of the Holy Ghost
within him. When, therefore, sin rises within
you, be not discouraged; its motions belong to
death, you to *life*. In such moments, turn to
Him who is the AUTHOR of your life ; and the
flesh, like winter's snow beneath the sun of
Spring, will melt away. Remember the promise is not—the "flesh" will become spirit, but
that SIN SHALL NOT HAVE DOMINION
OVER YOU.

Cheer up, then, my brother; be of good heart
Christ is not only your Redeemer, He is your
VICTORY in every contest with sin. To Him,
and to Him alone, *look* when sin, the " body of

this death," presses upon you, and your *deliverance is sure.* Above all, take this " strong consolation " for your comfort :—" THANKS BE UNTO GOD, WHICH ALWAYS CAUSETH US TO TRIUMPH IN CHRIST."—2 Cor. ii. 14.

In conclusion, dear reader, let me urge you afresh to come to your Lord and Master for grace and strength to help in every time of need. To encourage you to do so, let me bring before you some of God's " ABLES," all of which are yours in Christ :—

" ABLE to save them to the uttermost that come unto God by Him, seeing He ever liveth to make intercession for them."—*Heb.* vii. 25.

" ABLE to succour them that are tempted."— *Heb.* ii. 18.

" ABLE to do exceeding abundantly above all that we ask or think, according to the power that worketh in us."—*Eph.* iii. 20.

" ABLE even to subdue all things unto Himself." —Phill. iii. 21.

" ABLE to make all grace abound toward you; that ye, always having all sufficiency in all things, may abound to every good work."— 2 *Cor.* ix. 8.

" ABLE to keep you from falling, and to present you *faultless* before the presence of His glory, with exceeding joy."—*Jude* 24.

" ABLE to keep that which I have committed unto Him."—*2 Tim.* i. 12.

Such then are some of the exceeding great and precious promises ; and if, dear believer, you will only plead them at the throne of God, the *broken cable* will soon be restored, and you yourself be brought into FULL COMMUNION WITH THE FATHER AND WITH HIS SON JESUS CHRIST.

Lightning Source UK Ltd.
Milton Keynes UK
UKOW040000230112

185825UK00009B/4/P